ONE OF THE EXPERTS EXPLAIN SERIES - THERE ARE OTHERS!

The last 'showman's engine to be made. This magnificent example, 'Supreme' (they all had names) was built in 1934 by John Fowler. The engine weighs about 25 tonnes and carries 2 300 litres (say 500 gallons) of water and almost half a tonne of coal. On the road it is limited to a speed of 12 miles an hour but can go considerably faster. In earlier days, Supreme would tow a train of heavy caravans to the fairground, then turn into a generating station to power bumper cars, lighting and so on. It still makes regular appearances at steam fairs. The great Supreme belongs to Jack Wharton, President of the National Traction Engine Club.

'Supreme' lit up at night. Photo by Ivan Belcher

STEAM-THE ATMOSPHERE AND YOU

Today everybody thinks of steam power as coming from pressure – steam pushing pistons forward and back, or jetting onto the blades of rotors to spin them at high speeds.

But in the first days of steam, pressure was not a possibility partly because nobody could make a boiler that was strong enough; the pressure would force leaks or explode the boiler.

So the earliest engines depended not on the pressure built up inside themselves, but on the pressure outside – the pressure of the atmosphere. This pressure, which acts on everyone and everything on our earth is the same as a column of water about 9 metres high; anyone who has swum near the bottom at the deep end of a swimming pool (Little more than a mere 2 m) will be able to imagine the weight of the load bearing down on us. Actually, the weight of the whole atmosphere has been worked out at about 5 000 million million tonnes – an astonishing thought. We only survive this big squeeze because the pressure inside us equals the pressure outside.

A very small amount of heated water can create a very large amount of steam; to be precise, one 'part' of water at its boiling point makes 1 300 'parts' of steam – an enormous expansion.

Prove the crushing power of the atmosphere

This is a very simple experiment but young people should not try it without an adult present.

Take a well made tin with a separate, press-on lid. On *no* account use a tin with a screw-on or other fixed lid. Put about 1 cm of water in the bottom of the tin and rest the lid in place – do *not* press it down. Light a low gas under tin and wait until the water is boiling and steam coming quite strongly out. Then, using heat-proof gloves, turn out the gas, press the lid firmly down to make an airtight seal, then drop the tin into a sink or big saucepan of cold water. Now the steam which was filling the whole tin will condense back into the small amount of water, leaving a partial vacuum. The pressure inside no longer equals the pressure outside and the tin will crumple.

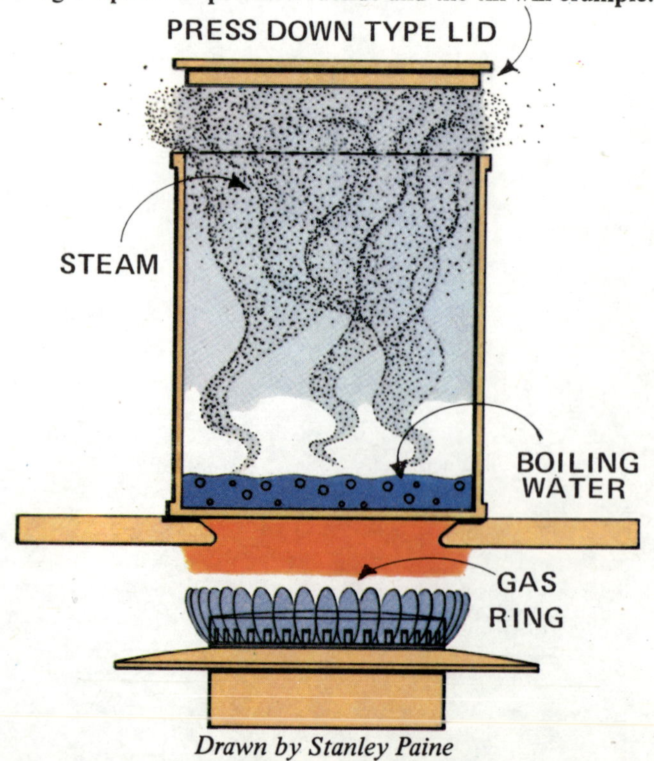

Drawn by Stanley Paine

CYLINDER

PISTON

A brilliant German experimenter, Otto von Guericke, built a cylinder and snugly fitting piston in 1654. He pumped air out from under the piston and challenged 50 men to haul on ropes to stop the piston being sucked down into the partial vacuum. Guericke won the contest – by having atmospheric pressure on his side. This was to set people thinking about steam and how it could cause a vacuum which could be made to work.

Denis Papin tests steam power

Thinking time in the sixteen hundreds tended to be prolonged! Thirty-six years after Guericke's experiment a Frenchman, Denis Papin used steam – and the pressure of the atmosphere – to move a piston. In 1690, he made a little brass cylinder about 60 mm in diameter and put water, then a piston into it. Steam lifted the piston and it was held in the 'up' position by a catch. Then a weight was hung from the piston and the fire removed. As Papin expected, the steam condensed back into water, caused a partial vacuum and, when he released the catch, the piston plunged down lifting the weight. That was as far as he took his experiment and another long pause for thought set in.

SCHOOL PROJECT

This practical experiment will be beyond the capacity of young people unless they have adult help and proper facilities.

USE PAPIN'S IDEA TO MAKE A PUMPING ENGINE

This 'atmospheric' cylinder and piston will have to be made up by someone equipped with metal working tools, probably a toolmaker. (Ours was made by F. West of Riverside Motors, 139 Lee Road, London SE3).

THE CYLINDER Brass tube 50 mm diameter, thickness, 3 mm. Base is 5 mm thick brass press fitted into the base, then silver soldered.

PISTON Solid brass turned in a lathe to '2 thou' undersize. Two slots are cut (by turning in a lathe) and these 'rings' are packed with square, graphited asbestos. A coating of oil above the piston may make a good enough seal without the rings and packing.

FILLER PLUG Brass, screw-in type. A thread will have to be cut into the cylinder base. It is better to fit the plug with a heat resistant washer.

THE EXPERIMENT Suspend the cylinder in a framework – we used Meccano. Make sure the piston can move freely. Remove the filler plug and put in small quantity of water. Heat the base of the cylinder.

When the steam forms and pushes the piston to the top of the cylinder, remove the heat and squirt cold water at the cylinder.

When the steam condenses watch the piston drive strongly downwards. If you attach it to a cord running over a pulley it will lift quite a heavy weight.

1 Dan (left) takes the weight of the 'beam' and 'pump rods' while Ben (right) pulls the piston out to show its rings and graphited asbestos packing. All the engine parts can be seen.

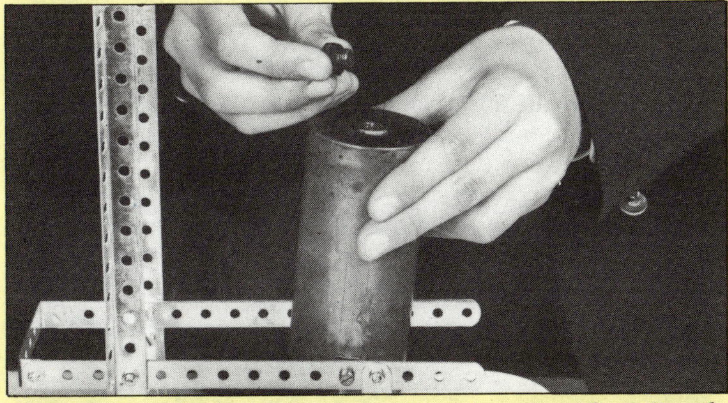

2 Ben makes the first move to get the engine going – he swings the cylinder up and takes the filler plug out. A cup of cold water is beside him.

3 The piston is about 1 cm clear of the cylinder's base, and now Ben uses a dropper to fill the space with water. A medical syringe is even easier to use. Always fill to the brim.

WORKING STEAM ENGINES AT LAST

Papin's work with the little brass cylinder was written up seven years after he made the experiment – in 1697. An Englishman from Devon, Thomas Newcomen, may or may not have read the report, but at about that time he began work on an engine using steam on the same lines as the Frenchman. The difference was, a real engine and its task was to pump water out of mines in neighbouring Cornwall.

Newcomen, a modest but determined man, slogged on for about 15 years before his first engine was ready. Then it was not in Cornwall that it was put to work, but in Staffordshire.
Apart from the many mechanical difficulties Newcomen had to deal with was the awkward fact that anoth[er] Thomas, Thomas Savery, had already patented a steam engine for pumping water. Savery used the steam vacuum idea to suck water up to a tank, then modest steam pressure to blow it on up to the discharge pipe. His engine – he called it *The Miner's Friend* – certainly worked, but only up to a point, and with frequent breakdowns. Savery's engine had no piston; but

SCHOOL PROJECT continued

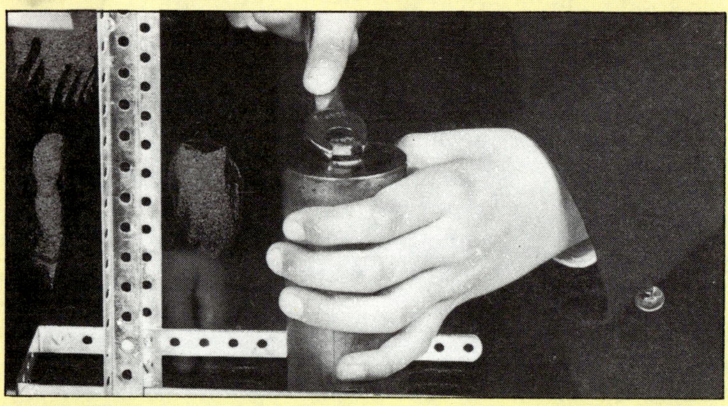

4 Ben tightens the filler plug and will swing the cylinder down to its working position. Then he fixes the string from the piston rod to a hook on the beam.

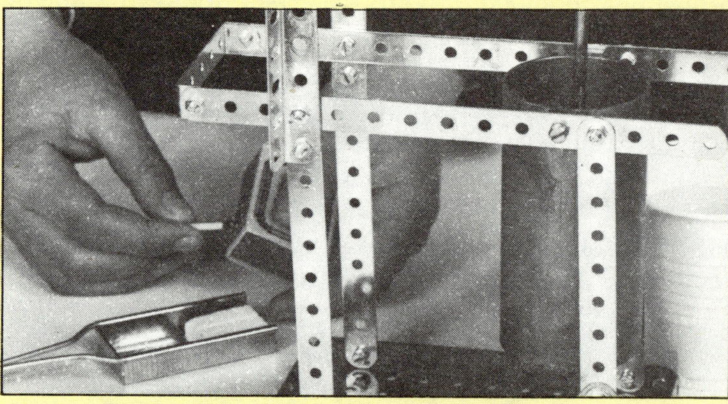

5 Dan lights a tablet of Mamod's solid fuel in a fire tray and places the flame beneath the cylinder. Both boys watch for the cylinder to rise as steam expands to push it up.

6 The piston is up and the 'pump rods' down. Ben removes the fire and Dan, who has filled the dropper (or syringe) with cold water, squirts the cylinder to cool it and condense the steam.

7 A vacuum has caused the piston to plunge down pulling the rods up which in real life could be pumping water from a mine. Atmospheric pressure does the work. The cycle is repeated.

Chelsea Water Works in the 1750 s. A Newcomen-type beam engine did the pumping. *Photo: Science Museum*

even so his patents were so broad that they would have blocked Newcomen. The inventive Newcomen solved that by going into partnership with the other man.

The main parts of Newcomen's engine (see drawing on page 6) were a boiler to make steam, a cylinder above it containing a piston and, looming over the whole thing, a massive wooden beam balanced on a wall and pivoting like a see-saw. One end of the beam was connected by chain to the piston, the other to heavy pump rods — rather like colossal bicycle pumps — which hung down in the mine. Steam was condensed by a squirt of cold water in the cylinder and the partial vacuum pulled the piston and one end of the beam down; the other end went up and pumped the mine water clear; then the weight of the rods rocked the beam the other way to lift the piston for the next working stroke.

Newcomen's engine was built in 1712 — and was an astounding success, lifting 2,275 litres of water (say 500 gallons) 50 m *every minute,* year in and year out. *The action was very slow — one power stroke to the piston about every five seconds.* Nevertheless, Newcomen's design was so good it went almost unchanged for more than half a century. Two hundred or more machines were built and quite a few exported. They had an important effect on Britain's economy making flooded mines workable and taking water supplies to towns. Sadly, Newcomen was cheated out of most of the profit and fame that should have been his.

Two weaknesses

Great though Newcomen's engines were there were two big design problems he never solved. One was that the jet of cold water which condensed the steam also cooled the boiler — which had to be heated up again by the next intake of steam, some of which was therefore wasted. The other was that *because the end of the beam rocked through an arc it could not be rigidly fixed to the piston* — the piston could pull by a chain but it was not able to push back; the weight of the rods had to deal with that part of the see-saw action.

Both these limitations were solved by the great James Watt

James Watt, problem solver

James Watt, born in Scotland in 1736, was an extraordinary man by any standard. He was a brilliant engineer and inventor, a man of vision who sometimes showed a disappointing lack of it, he was stubborn, ambitious, mean to his assistants, humourless, and given to complaining about his health though he lived to be 83 – a rare ripe old age for his time. At least he did win the fame and recognition denied to Newcomen – and decidedly he deserved it. Watt was an engineering genius.

He spent some years as an instrument maker working for Glasgow University and, as it happened, the university owned a model Newcomen engine which needed attention. Watt was asked to deal with it. He became intrigued by the action of the little atmospheric engine and quickly saw what was wrong. The repeated cooling of the cylinder when condensing the steam stopped it from running well. Although he spotted the trouble quickly it seems to have taken him a long time to see the cure. Then it came

James Watt *Photo: Science Museum*

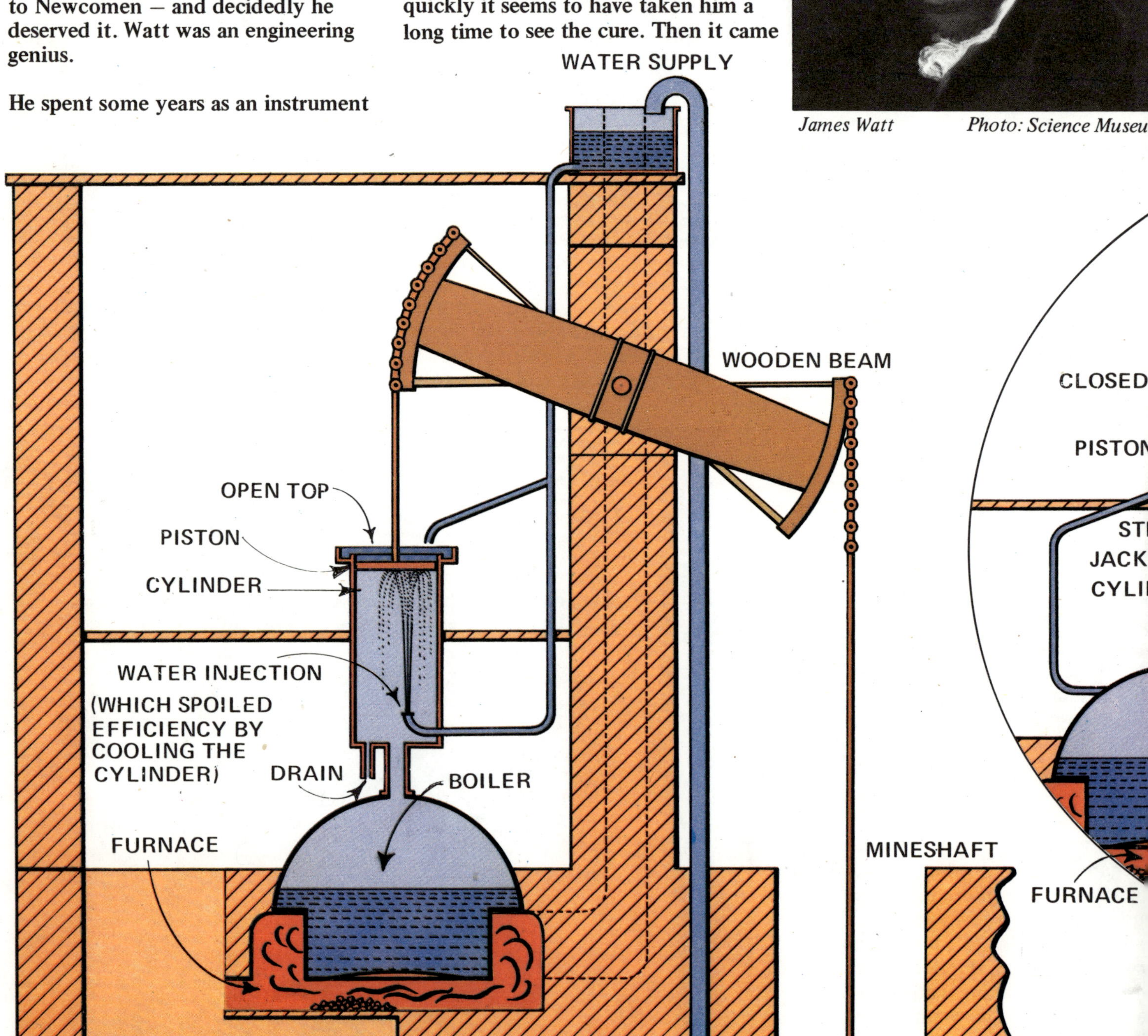

1 NEWCOMEN'S ATMOSPHERIC STEAM ENGINE FOR DRAINING MINES

to him when he was out for a Sunday walk: get the steam out of the cylinder and condense it somewhere else. But how? His answer: a separate tank submerged in water to keep it cool, connect it to the cylinder by a pipe incorporating a valve (or tap), pump air from the tank, turn the valve to 'on' and, when the steam rushes into the tank condense it there with the usual cold water jet. The idea worked and Watt was on his way to becoming world-famous. He patented his separate condenser in 1769 when he was only 33.

At about the same time he made other

CUGNOT'S THREE-WHEELED STEAM CARRIAGE

At the same time as Watt patented his separate condenser, a young Frenchman, Nicholas Cugnot, demonstrated a three-wheeled steam carriage in Paris. It reached 2 miles per hour. He followed it with an improved version using government money. On its first outing the new carriage capsized. Cugnot was sent to jail.

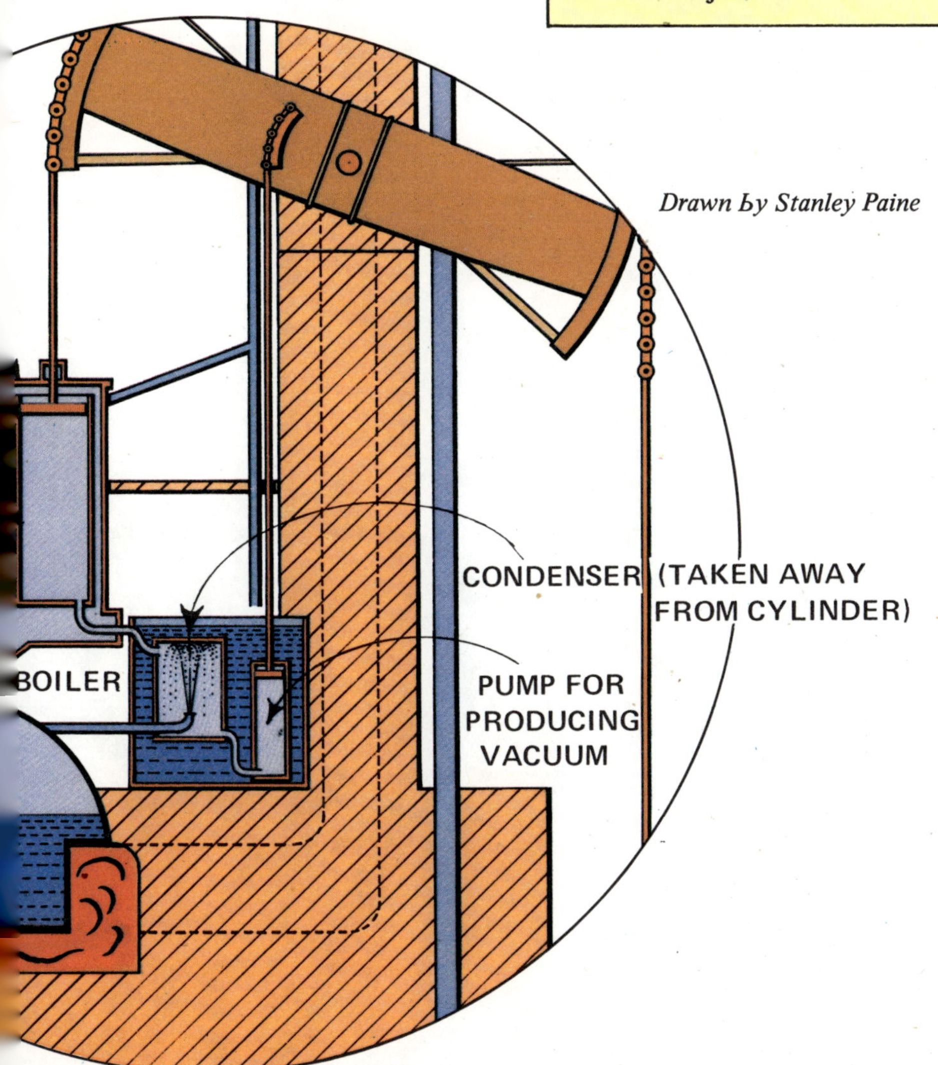

Drawn by Stanley Paine

2 JAMES WATT'S IMPROVED ATMOSPHERIC STEAM ENGINE

The main difference between Newcomen's engine and Watt's was the separate condenser. Now when steam was cooled to create a vacuum, the cylinder could remain hot. This drawing shows how Watt did it.

improvements – notably having steam under *slight* pressure pushing on one side of the piston while the usual vacuum 'sucked' on the other. To contain the steam Watt had to close the top of the cylinder but let the connecting rod poke through without losing steam. Also he had to devise a more efficient fit of piston-to-cylinder; he thought out the equivalent of the modern car's piston ring – he made a groove round the rim of the piston and packed it with rope (hemp). Finally, he fitted a steam-filled jacket round the cylinder to keep it warm.

The result was an engine four times as efficient as the Newcomen type and so cheaper to run. But between designing

PUSH PULL PISTONS NEEDED A NEW TYPE OF CONNECTION TO THE BEAM. SEE OVER THE PAGE

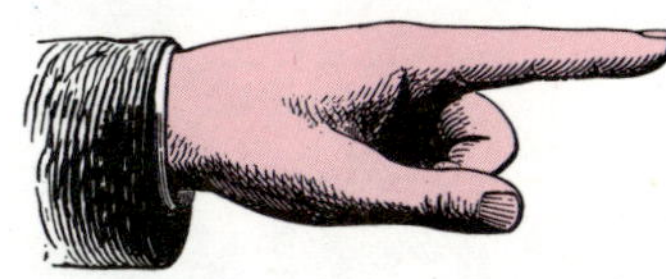

HOW WATT CAME UP WITH WHAT HE DESCRIBED AS HIS 'MOST ELEGANT' INVENTION.

But Watt continued to think up new ideas

Continued from page 7

his new engine and being able to put it on the market came another very long pause – six years. The reason was a mixture of money troubles and the inability and mechanics to work as accurately as he required.

Watt was now in partnership with a very able manufacturer and business-man, Matthew Boulton. Boulton and Watt engines became quickly well known and the demand for them was huge.

In the early 1780's, Watt made huge advances with his steam engines. He made his pistons 'double acting' – meaning they pushed as well as pulling which gave twice the power from the same sized cylinder, and he attached his overhead beam to a flywheel instead of the simple pump.
SO STEAM MOVED INTO WHAT IS KNOWN AS THE 'ROTATIVE ENGINE' PHASE.
But making pistons push the beam brought a new problem – how to connect the vertical action of the piston rod with the arcing action of the beam. Chains were now out of date.

Watt was prodded by his partner Boulton into developing engines that turned wheels instead of merely pumping. This is an engine he made in 1788. The piston pushed as well as pulling and Watt devised his 'parallel beam' link between the piston rod and overhead beam. This linkage was used for over 100 years.

Photo: Science Museum

Make a cardboard model of Watt's 'Parallel Motion' Linkage

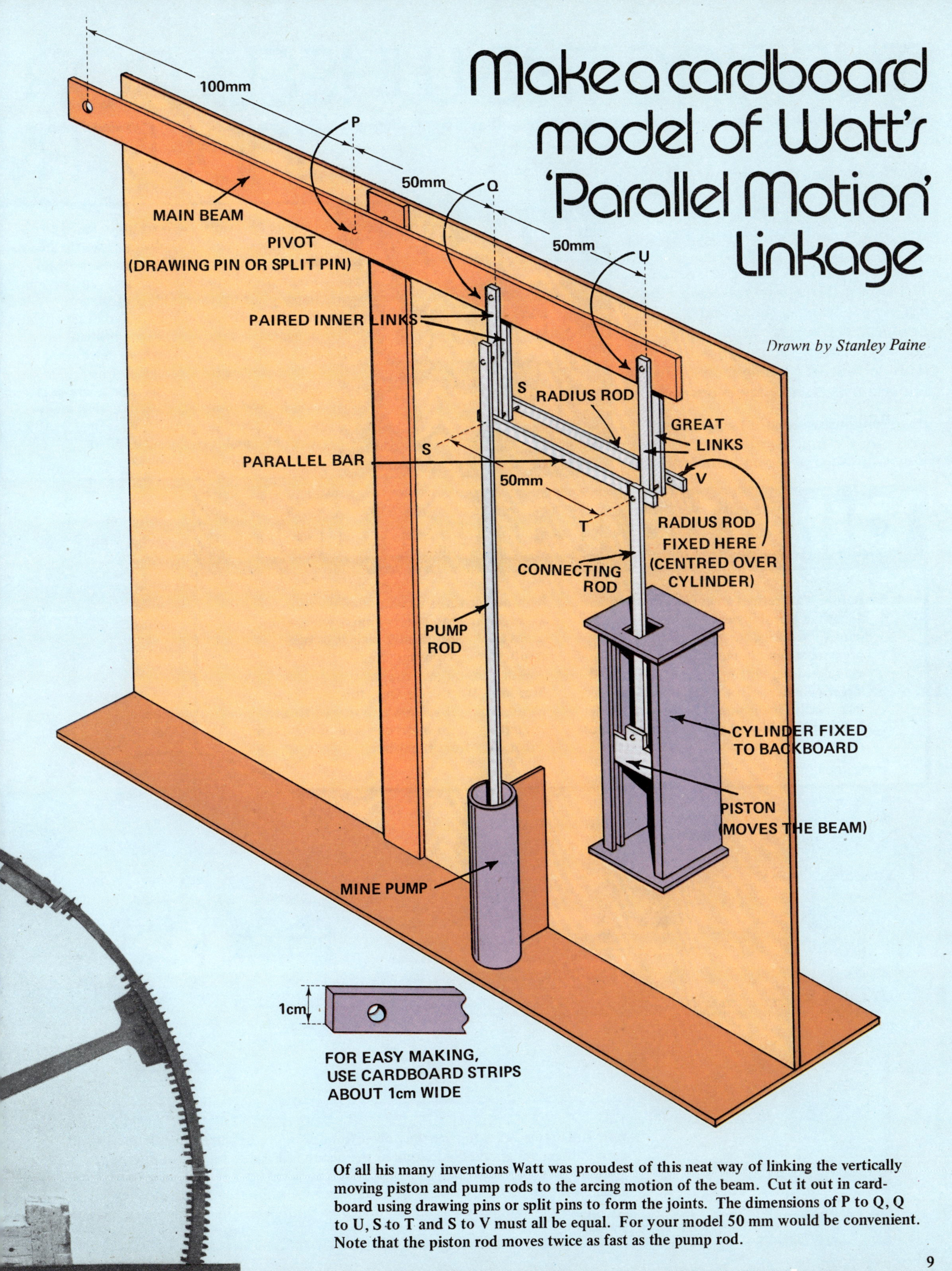

Drawn by Stanley Paine

Of all his many inventions Watt was proudest of this neat way of linking the vertically moving piston and pump rods to the arcing motion of the beam. Cut it out in cardboard using drawing pins or split pins to form the joints. The dimensions of P to Q, Q to U, S to T and S to V must all be equal. For your model 50 mm would be convenient. Note that the piston rod moves twice as fast as the pump rod.

TURNING THE WHEELS FOR INDUSTRY

The success of Watt's rotary engines was immediate – they utterly changed the way industry worked. And his ideas kept flowing.

Besides the separate condenser, the double acting piston, the steam jacket and the famous parallel bars link, Watt developed a new way of saving steam. He used it 'expansively'. That simply means that *before* the piston has moved through its full stroke the supply of steam to the cylinder is stopped. The steam *continues* to expand, pushing the piston before it. This cutting off became more and more important as steam engines developed.

Beam engines were still being built well into the nineteen hundreds because they were so simple and trouble free.

Despite his brilliance, Watt quite failed to see some of the (now) obvious uses for steam. He opposed the use of high pressure steam – which he held to be dangerous – and he was fiercely against the building of 'steam carriages'. He was also unfair to other engine designers and even to his own brilliant assistant, William Murdock, whom he stopped from developing a steam-driven three-wheeler. He spent a lot of time going to law over his wide-ranging patents and in many ways hindered progress. Watt retired in 1800, when his condenser patent expired.

Other basic inventions

Before Watt retired an engineer named Jonathan Hornblower took the idea of 'expansive' working further by letting high pressure steam do part of its work in a small cylinder, then putting it through a second, larger cylinder, while it still had some energy left. Sadly, the jealous Watt stopped him because Hornblower was using his condenser, (patents again) but the idea went on and became known as a compound engine. Later, more than two cylinders were sometimes used. Spectacular savings in fuel resulted from compounding.
Another important invention came from Murdock, Watt's assistant: this was the so-called sliding D-valve which moved to and fro letting steam in on one side of the piston exhausting from the other.

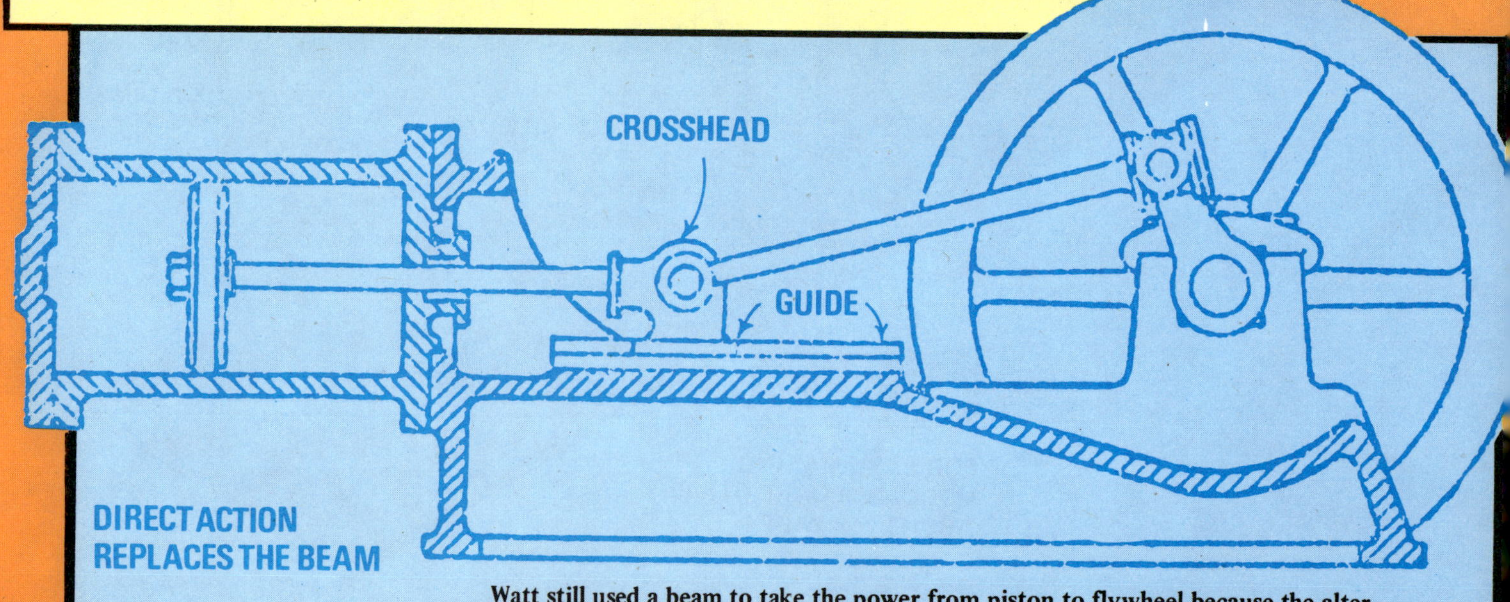

DIRECT ACTION REPLACES THE BEAM

Watt still used a beam to take the power from piston to flywheel because the alternative 'direct action' method required the piston rod end to be guided by very accurate rods, or a slide. These were difficult to make until steel planing came along in about 1820. An iron or steel 'crosshead' fixed to the piston rod end slid up and down the guide rods and was linked to the flywheel by a connecting rod and crank.

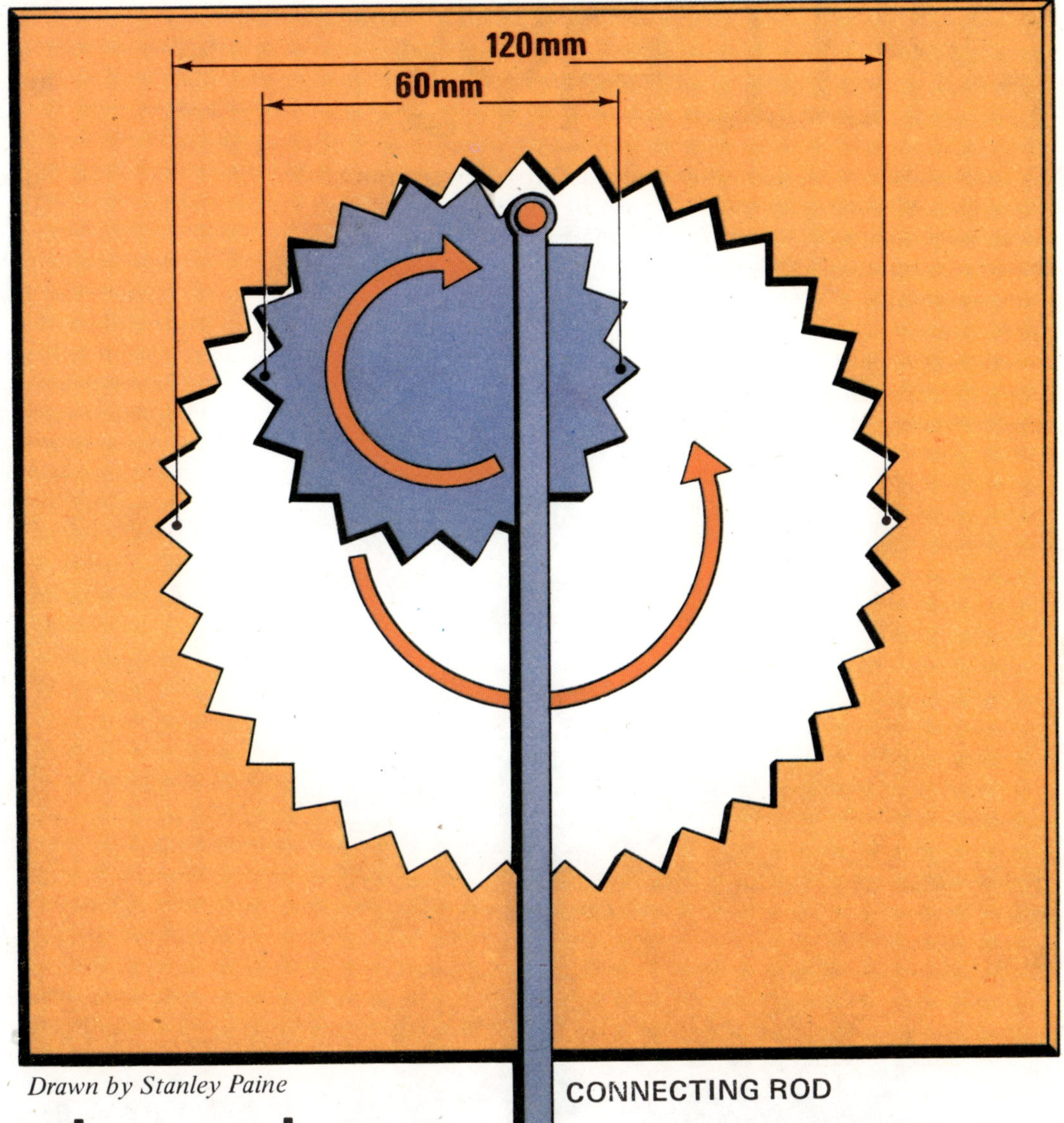

Drawn by Stanley Paine

Another and neat way of converting the up and down movement of the piston into a rotary motion

Cut this out in cardboard – forget the teeth – and test the idea. If the smaller wheel is half the diameter of the rim it sits inside, the piston rod will go vertically up and down as the wheel turns. In practice, of course, it was the other way round – the piston rod moved the wheel. This was Murray's Cycloidal Engine. The theory was fine but the teeth had a very short life.

BUT A MAN DUE TO BECOME AS FAMOUS AS WATT WAS ALSO AT WORK

THIS WAS RICHARD TREVITHICK, ACTIVE NEAR THE END OF THE SEVENTEEN HUNDREDS. HE MADE STEAM MOVE IN A BIG WAY BY PUTTING IT ON RAILS.

MAKING STEAM MOVE

Steam on the move
RAILWAYS

Locomotive design which started with Richard Trevithick in 1803 went on until the 1940's. There were many characters, larger-than-life men involved through the whole period.

Trevithick was as much a pioneer as Newcomen – and equally unrecognised in his time. His strangely beautiful engine built at Pen-y-darran ironworks, South Wales, hauled 10 tons of iron ore for 10 miles in 1804 and, in doing so, cost a rival ironworks owner 500 guineas (£525) who had laid a bet with Trevithick's sponsor it would fail. Even so, and although Trevithick built other improved engines, he had no real success. Yet he had put together some important 'firsts'. He used high pressure steam, put exhaust steam up the chimney which sucked air through the fire to make it burn hotter, and ran the engine on rails. These design points were copied by later engineers.

One of the earliest of all railway locomotives – built at Pen-y-darran Ironworks in 1804.

Photo: Science Museum

Richard Trevithick, a man ahead of his time.
Photo: Science Museum

'Trevithick's engines were everywhere: put one in a building and it was industrial; put it on wheels and it was a locomotive; put it in a ship and you had a dredger'
(Quote, a Science Museum expert)

The most famous early engine is George Stephenson's Rocket. It was built in 1829 – and had just about everything right that matters. The Rocket had its

(Continued on page 16)

FLYING SCOTSMAN

The world's most famous locomotive, the Flying Scotsman was built in 1923 and made her last 'for real' run in 1963. She is a Pacific class, 4-6-2 locomotive designed by Sir Nigel Gresley. When diesel power came in British Rail were hostile to the idea of preserving steam locomotives and allowing them to run on their railway system. Happily, Alan Pegler, a businessman with a passion for steam locomotives, managed to buy the Flying Scotsman and preserve her.

She was expensive to maintain and in an effort to make her earn her keep he took her to the US for demonstration runs in 1969.

The tour was not a success from the point of view of making money.

The Flying Scotsman was on the point of going under the hammer to pay off debts when William McAlpine, like Pegler, a steam enthusiast, offered to buy the engine and bring her back to Britain. In the nick of time it was done, George Hinchcliffe (who runs the Steamtown Railway Museum at Carnforth) doing the negotiating. The Flying Scotsman, No 4472, is parked now at Carnforth, Lancashire. She gets up steam during the better-weather months and goes touring pulling trainloads of enthusiasts.

Photo: Tom Boustead

Although she was built back in 1923 the Flying Scotsman can still reach 100 mph – but these days British Rail restrict her to a measly 60. She looks and is in beautiful condition, cared for by George Hinchcliffe who tells how to drive the engine on page 15.

THE FLYING SCOTSMAN
No. 4472

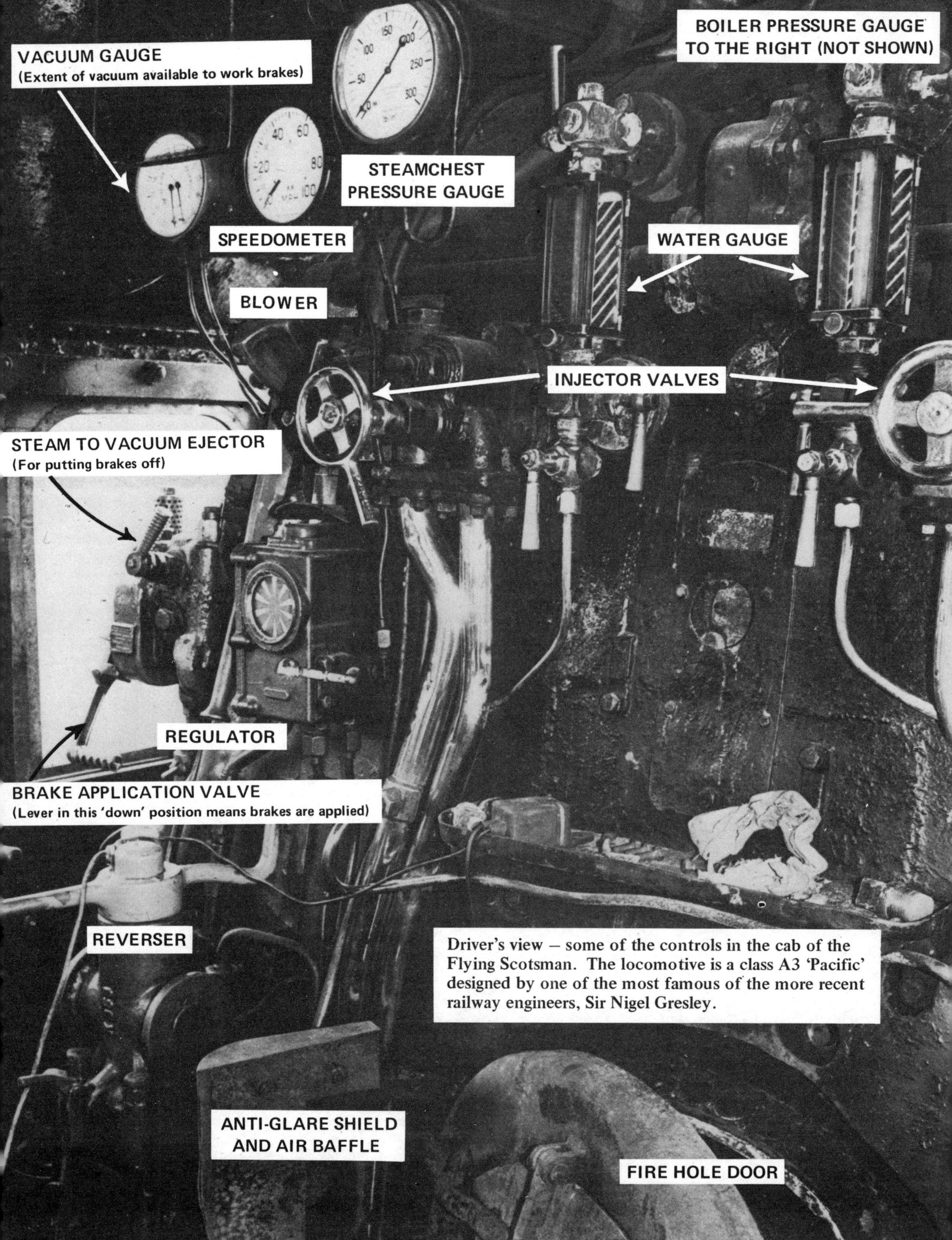

Driver's view – some of the controls in the cab of the Flying Scotsman. The locomotive is a class A3 'Pacific' designed by one of the most famous of the more recent railway engineers, Sir Nigel Gresley.

EXCLUSIVE

How to drive the Flying Scotsman

Photo: Tom Boustead

The Flying Scotsman has three cylinders. The two outside ones are connected directly to the centre driving wheels. Drive is then passed by coupling rods to the rest of the main wheels. A third cylinder centrally between the frames and under the smokebox drives the centre pair of main wheels – the piston rod is connected to a crank in the centre axle and is out of sight.

Despite its massive size the Flying Scotsman is fairly simple to drive. It was hard work for the fireman who probably had to load eight tons of coal from the tender to the fire between London and Edinburgh.

RAISING STEAM

First the boiler must have water – it should show half way up the gauge glass.

Put dry wood, a small amount of coal and a couple of fire lighters into the firegrate. Follow with rag soaked in paraffin which are put on a shovel, lit and among the wood and coal. As the fire catches, put on more coal.

To get 40 lbs (per sq in) or steam up takes about 5 hours. Then turn on the blower (jets of steam) and the fire burns brighter and hotter. To take steam pressure on

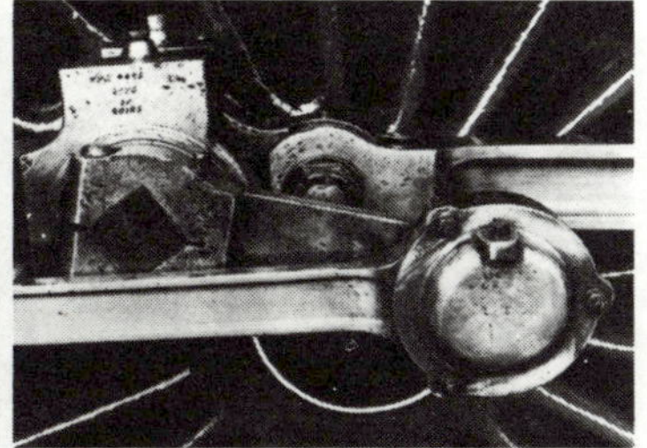

up to 220 lbs takes only 30 more minutes. While getting up steam the driver goes round oiling over 100 lubrication points on the engine.

Look at the basic controls – some show in the picture opposite. There is a hand brake on the ten-

der; a reverser which controls the steam flow to make the engine go forward or backwards; a regulator – rather like a car's accelerator – starts the engine and the wider it is opened the more power is given; the vacuum brake valve puts the brakes on the wheels of the engine and carriages; injectors jet new water into the boiler (from the tender) as steam is made and used.

READY TO MOVE

Open the steam-to-vacuum-ejector valve to take the brakes off; put the engine into forward gear by turning the reverser; open the regulator – but gently, or the wheels will slip. The Flying Scotsman is rolling!

SAVING STEAM

Before the piston has travelled its full stroke steam can be cut off and will carry on expanding energetically. This is done with the reverser. Cut-off is given as a percentage. A cut-off of 50% means the piston in the cylinder has travelled half its stroke when the steam supply is stopped. A so-called piston valve does the stopping – it moves backwards and forwards in a small cylinder of its own which steam must pass through on its way to the main cylinder.

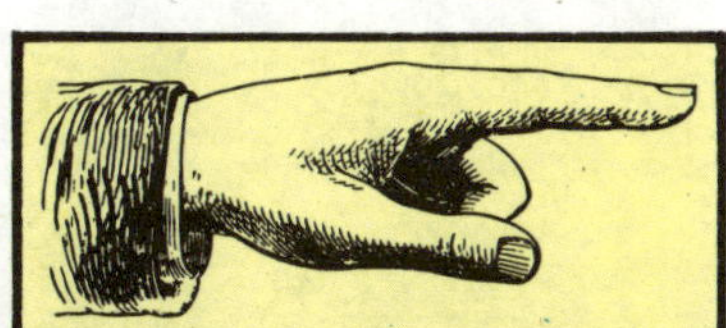

A drawing on pages 20 and 21 shows how tubes carried flames and hot gases through the boiler of a traction engine. The same method of turning water into steam was used on steam locomotives.

GETTING THE FLYING SCOTSMAN FLYING

The Flying Scotsman does its fastest and most economical work when the *regulator* is wide open and the *reverser* set to give a cut-off of 15% to 18%.

NOW STOP

To stop, close the regulator and press the brake application valve. Now brake shoes clamp onto the wheels. There is as much skill in stopping a train smoothly as in starting it.

THE FIREMAN'S PART

The fireman keeps the steam pressure up by stoking the fire, and by working the injectors to

replenish water used up as steam. The injector allows a jet of water and a jet of steam to combine – so the water is literally blown into the boiler at high speed against the pressure of steam and water already in.

SHUTTING DOWN

To shut the engine down fill the boiler until the injectors stop, let the fire die, drop part of the grate which lets the fire and hot ash fall into a pan – then shovel into a pit. The smokebox door (at the front) is opened and ashes and soot taken out by shovel. Leave the tender brake on.

But there were many other great locomotives besides the Flying Scotsman

THE ENGINE THAT TAUGHT LOCOMOTIVE DESIGNERS ALL THE RIGHT PRINCIPLES

Before Stephenson had built his first steam locomotive, the famous Puffing Billy was at work in Newcastle, hauling coal. At that time people doubted whether smooth wheels would get a good enough grip on smooth rails – Puffing Billy proved they were wrong. It was built by William Hedley and Christopher Blackett in 1813.

Photo: Science Museum

firebox as an extension of the boiler so it could be partly jacketed by water, the flames and hot gases passed through small tubes surrounded by water in the boiler (very efficient), steam came out of the 'blast pipe' into the funnel to draw air through the fire (Trevithick's idea), the cylinders were outside the boiler and there was direct drive to the wheels by means of sliding cross-heads and connecting rods. It also pulled a tender with supplies of water and coal.

The Rocket had almost everything, but not quite. Stephenson took the next steps just a year later (in 1830) with his 'Northumbrian'. It had the firebox tucked fully inside the boiler (even more efficient), cylinders horizontal (almost) and a smokebox at the front which caught ashes and soot – and added to the strength of the whole engine.

Later steam locomotives were bigger, had more wheels and used coupling rods to spread the driving power from wheel to wheel. But essentially they were just the 'Rocket' and 'Northumbrian' improved.

George Stephenson, helped by his son Robert, built the first steam-powered public railway – in 1825 four years before the Rocket appeared. This was the Stockton and Darlington Railway. George drove the engine named Locomotion on the opening day. Locomotion hauled coal, freight and hundreds of passengers. But it had the cylinders in the top of the boiler and complicated linkages to the driving wheels; not as good a design as the Rocket. The opening of the railway made the Stephensons world-famous and gave Britain a strong lead in railway design and construction.

This pretty looking London & North Western Railway 2-4-0 'Hardwick' was built in 1892. After being restored by the National Railway Museum it hauled a train from Crewe to Carlisle at 67 miles an hour. Hardwick is said to be capable of 90 miles an hour.

Photo: John Everit

The famous 4-4-2 Atlantic class came before the Flying Scotsman and other 'Pacifics'. They were designed by Harry Ivatt, were very successful and were among the first of the really modern looking locomotives.

Photos: National Railway Museum, York

Patrick Stirling's 'Eight footer' built at Doncaster in 1870 and known by that name because the driving wheel has a diameter of 8 feet. Stirling and some other designers thought it best to have a single pair of driving wheels for high speed trains, so the wheels had to be very large. The 'Eight footer' is preserved at the National Railway Museum at York. Stirling and other designers tended to be opinionated – he opposed visible coupling rods because he thought they looked unsightly.

Locomotives are described by the arrangement of their wheels. The Flying Scotsman has four 'bogies' in front, six driving wheels and two small trailing wheels, so she is a 4-6-2.

The 'ROCKET' – the world's most famous engine. It won a competition against other locomotives in 1829 and could do 29 mph.

AND THE MAN WHO BUILT THE 'ROCKET' – AND WHOLE RAILWAY SYSTEMS. GEORGE STEPHENSON.

His son Robert also became a great railway engineer.

Photo: Science Museum

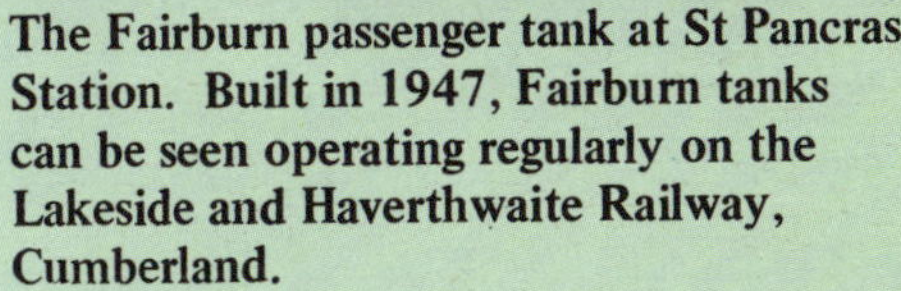

The Fairburn passenger tank at St Pancras Station. Built in 1947, Fairburn tanks can be seen operating regularly on the Lakeside and Haverthwaite Railway, Cumberland.

Superheating of steam was an important development. It means separating the steam from the water in the boiler and raising its temperature much above boiling point. It has vastly greater expansive power. Superheating is dealt with in the Experts Explain book on locomotives.

A Class A2 locomotive, 'Tudor Minstrel', working hard uphill approaching Riccarton Junction in Scotland. The A2s had a 4-6-2 wheel arrangement representing the final development of the LNER Pacific design. 'Blue Peter', a working example of the A2, has been preserved by the Blue Peter Preservation Society.

Photo: John Everitt

One of the proudest names in traction engine building – Burrell. This is 'Defiance' in close-up. It is a 4 NHP (nominal horsepower), compound (twin cylinder) Burrell tractor, weighs 5 tonnes and was built in Thetford in 1913. It often appears at steam fairs.

STEAM ON THE ROAD

Although the Frenchman, Nicolas Cugnot made his steam 'car' move (just) as early as 1769 steam was late coming to the roads. Steam 'carriages' appeared – and, for the most part, rapidly disappeared in the 1820s and '30s.

A PICTURE OF WALTER HANCOCK'S STEAM CARRIAGE 'ENTERPRISE' IS ON PAGE 25. IT RAN BETTER THAN MOST.

But it was not until the 1850s that the first *useful* traction engines appeared, and by then steam locomotives were running at up to 60 mph. But when steam traction engines did make their latish appearance at least they did so majestically.

Another Burrell 4 NHP compound tractor in a hurry. Tractors were lighter than traction engines and allowed to go faster – five miles an hour instead of four!

TRACTION ENGINES - AND H

Steam traction engines (and rollers) were crudely but beautifully made. The moving parts were cast iron – used for cylinders, pistons and piston rings. To get the bore smooth the pistons would be rubbed to and fro in the cylinder with sand. Then the sand was washed out.

But these engines would work, and work *hard*, for 20 or 30 years and still be as good as new if properly cared for. Many were well cared for because a man could spend his whole working life in partnership with one engine.

The drawing here shows how coal and water were converted by a traction engine into power and movement. Note that the firebox is jacketed by water, that the flames pass through the boiler to the smoke box (as with steam locomotives) and that used steam went out up the funnel to help fan the flames.

Unlike steam locomotives, the engine remained high, perched on top of the boiler. The drive to the back wheels was by a train of gears. Another difference is the conspicuous flywheel – always on the left of the engine.

Traction engines used to have to do an

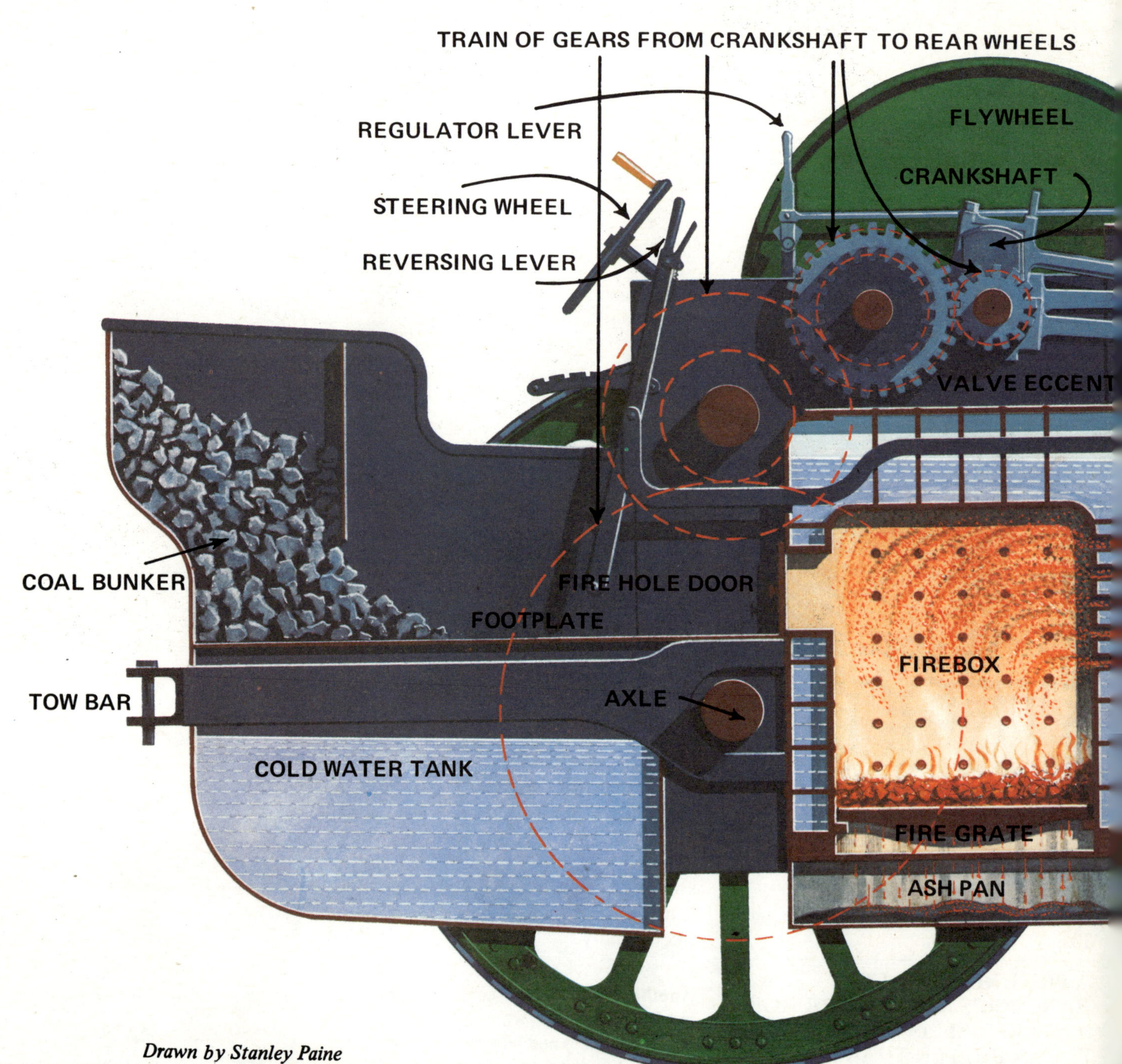

Drawn by Stanley Paine

OW THEY WORK

amazing variety of jobs. They would be coupled to manufacturing machinery by a long leather belt from the fly-wheel, would carry out general haulage (often a whole train of wagons) and they transformed farming taking the place of today's tractors, threshing and ploughing. Also, of course, there were Showmen's Engines for the fairground – huge and beautifully decorated

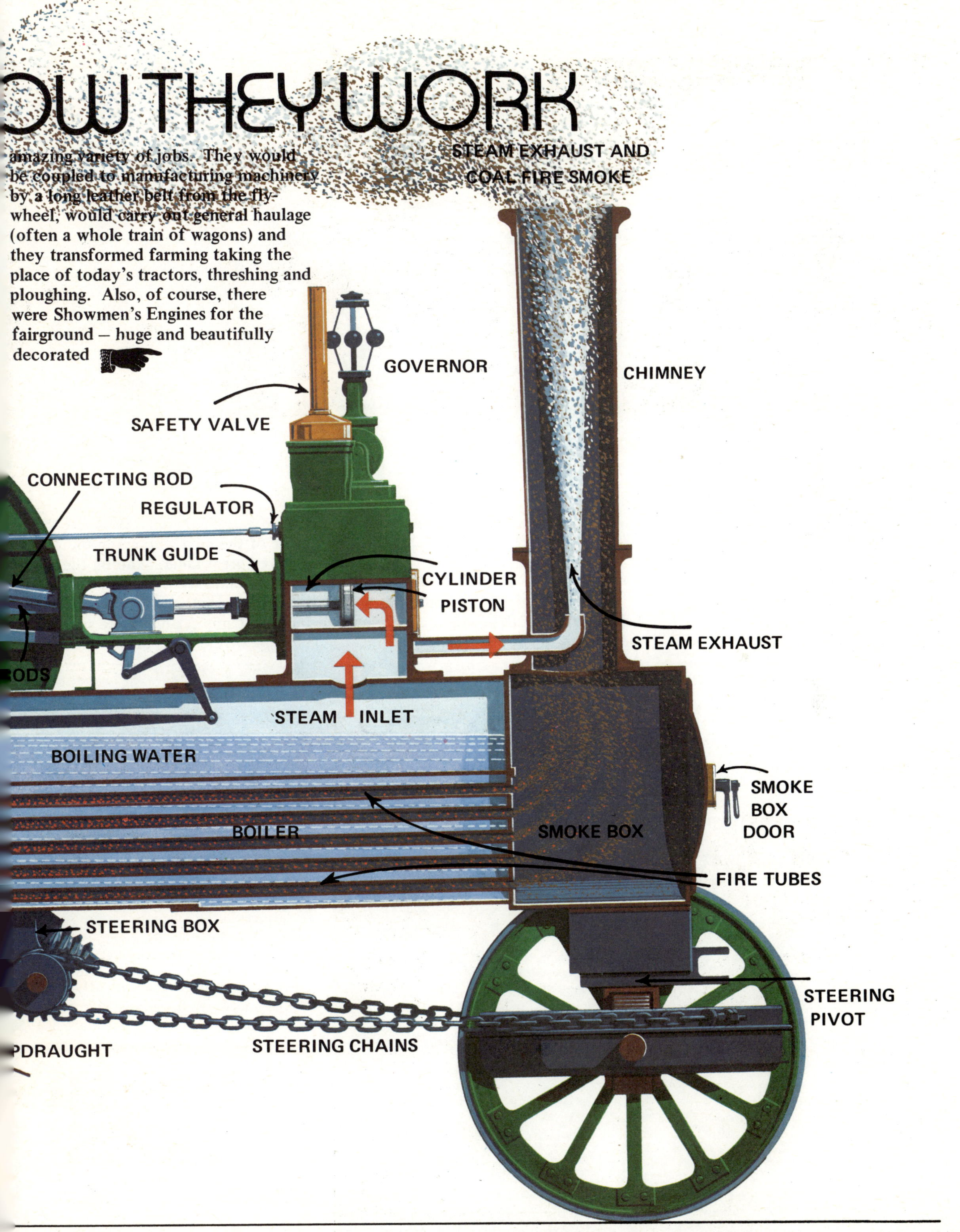

Above, an Aveling and Porter 4 NHP (nominal horsepower) tractor built in 1906 and owned, now, by Douglas Charlett of Yarnton.

Below, Jack Wharton's magnificent Fowler 10 NHP showman's engine, 'Supreme', built in 1934 and housed at Witney.

Continued from page 21

machines that pulled the cavalcade, then generated electrical power. Many thousands of engines were made between the 1860s and 1930s and some of the men who made them enjoyed great fame. Among the best known makes were Burrell, Fowler, Foden, Marshall and Aveling. One builder, Lampit, only made six engines but one of them has been preserved.

Above, 'Old Timer' owned by Arthur Nappe of Appleford. 'Old Timer' is a Marshall, 7 NHP single cylinder engine built in 1902; it won the first traction engine range in 195(

BURRELL'S TRICK

At first many people were suspicious of compound engines (two cylinders) so

Photos: *Ivan Belcher*

Above, 'Sarah' – a 5-ton Aveling and Porter 4 NHP compound tractor in a hurry. Owned by John Crawley.

DRIVING A MARSHALL TRACTION ENGINE

Check the gauge. Put rags on the fire shovel, pour on paraffin, and put a match to them. When the rags are well alight, place them through the fire hole into the middle of the fire box, add wood and, later, coal. As the coal burns, gently add more until the fire bars are covered with a thin layer of coal; this will reduce cold air drawn through the fire bars. Do not make a thick fire.

Above, another Marshall traction engine. This is the 6 NHP single cylinder model built in 1887. Owned by Jack Wharton of Witney. 'How to drive it' – see page 23.

Charles Burrell managed to make his compound engine look like a simple one. He linked the cylinders (one high pressure and the other low – using 'second hand' steam) to a single crank. Instead of being grateful for the better performance, some buyers were angry at being hoodwinked. In the 1900s compounding was widespread.

Photos: *Ivan Belcher*

GETTING UP STEAM

While the engine is getting up steam the driver lubricates the gears and axles and looks for loose nuts and missing split pins. At this stage the reversing lever should be in the middle position which makes it impossible for the engine to run. In about an hour steam should be up to working pressure. Before running the engine, make sure everything is clear of the moving parts, then open the cylinder drain taps to release any water (condensed steam) which has formed in the cylinder and steam chest.

NOW DRIVE IT

Run the engine for a while before making it drive. Now put the engine into gear, release the brake and put the reversing lever in the forward or rear position, depending on which way you want to go. Gently open the regulator and move off. Make sure all the 'condense' has gone from the cylinder, then close the cylinder drain taps.

YOU HAVE JUST BEEN DRIVING A TRACTION ENGINE

To stop can be difficult. Shut off steam, wind on the brake (a band grips the axle) and if you need to, go into reverse.

EXPLOSIONS

TRACTION ENGINES HAVE BEEN KNOWN TO EXPLODE BUT THIS CAN ONLY HAPPEN IF THE SAFETY VALVE IS JAMMED. THE MARSHALL WILL 'BLOW OFF' AT 150 LBS PER SQUARE INCH.

DOWNHILL DANGERS

Sometimes going downhill the water spills to the front of the boiler away from the firebox, which will then overheat. A lead plug should melt to let the water out (not too fast) and damp the fire. Too much water on the fire would cause a damaging explosion.

EARLY TRACTION ENGINE OWNERS AND DRIVERS WERE HOUNDED BY THE POLICE AND POLITICIANS

STEAM ON THE FARM

Photo: Ivan Belcher

The big challenge to engine builders was how to develop enough power to plough the land. A traction engine weighing maybe 10 tonnes was hard put to it to move over soft ground just

Photo: Colourviews

This Garrett, a steam driven ploughing engine did attempt to pull a plough directly – like modern tractors. It was cheerfully named 'Joker' but was soon overshadowed by petrol and diesel powered competition. 'Joker' was built in 1919 and is the only one left.

by itself, so expecting it to haul a massive plough digging deeply into the ground at the same time was too much – although many attempts were made of course. The makers were trying to imitate the direct pull of teams of horses.

But an enterprising 32-year-old engineer, John Fowler, showed a better way in 1858. He developed a long-boilered engine with two drums of wire hauser (or rope) slung underneath, and a quaint-looking plough with two sets of blades – when one set was digging the other was in the air. The traction engine moved into position, stopped, then

THIS WAY, SEE-SAW, THEN THAT WAY!

diverted its power to winding one drum which dragged the plough across the field turning up the soil. Next, the plough would be see-sawed to bring the unused blades down into the ground, the engine would move forward a width – and again stop. Now

PLOUGHING TEAMS OF TWO MEN AND A BOY WOULD MAKE THEIR SLOW WAY ROUND FROM FARM TO FARM DURING THE SEASON – WITH THEIR ENGINES, A PLOUGH AND A CARAVAN TO SLEEP IN.

it would wind the other drum which had its hauser passed round an anchor at the far end of the field to drag the plough on a return journey.

Fowler went one better in 1863 when he had two sister engines moving forward and stopping, and pulling the plough to and fro. The method was used for many, many years.

'Hero' – a McLaren ploughing engine. It works with another engine pulling the plough from one to the other, then moving forward to repeat the action. Shown here at a National Traction Engine Club event at Stourpaine, Dorset in 1975.

Walter Hancock's steam carriage of 1833, which ran better than some.

STEAM CARRIAGES APPEARED – AND SOMETIMES DISAPPEARED

ROLLING THE ROADS

At heart steam rollers are traction engines with a heavy roller replacing the front wheels. Many were actually convertible – they rolled in the winter and hauled in the summer.

In Britain, Aveling & Porter were the leading manufacturers and they built their last one in 1938. But most of the traction engine builders made them too – Burrell, Fowler and Marshall among them.

A Fowler 10 ton compound steam roller working hard. This is 'The Highlander' built in 1924. Owned by A D Hall of Brinfield.

Photo: Ivan Belcher

STEAM WAGONS

The drivers of steam wagons became uneasy if their journey took them too far away from streams or lakes; every few miles they had to sling their 'sucker' over the side to draw in fresh water from somewhere. A filter on the end stopped frogs, fishes and other foreign bodies from going into the tank.

DRIVERS HAD TO SHOVEL COAL FORWARD TO THE FURNACE TOO, FROM A COAL BUNKER JUST BEHIND THE CAB – SO THEY WERE BUSY MEN.

Even so, the steam wagon was a highly efficient lorry and van. Wagons came on the scene fairly late, were often cleverly designed and would probably still be in use today had they not been taxed out of existence by governments who favoured petrol and diesel-powered vehicles.

Above, rare specimen of a six-ton wagon built by the Yorkshire Steam Wagon Company in 1914. This one stood derelict for nearly 25 years but was gradually restored between 1958 and 1970.

Below, this Foden six-ton wagon is a youngster – built in 1925. It has a name, Emily. Like so many other steam wagons of many kinds it spent years as a derelict. In the early 1970s Emily was restored.

Photos: Ivan Belcher

Steam wagons were not fast – most cruised at from 12 to 20 miles an hour, but they had great power and very rapid acceleration. Compared to the thunderous juggernauts on the roads today they were wonderfully quiet.

STEAM WAGONS BECAME HIGHLY EFFICIENT IN THE 1930s BUT WERE TAXED OUT OF EXISTENCE. SOME PEOPLE ARE ASKING, WITH THE OIL CRISIS IN MIND, WILL THEY COME BACK?

Many steam wagons have been preserved and, like the two shown here, are regularly put on view at steam fairs.

Steam wagons were of two main types. First came what was little more than a traction engine with a deck for load carrying behind it; this the 'over-type' had the engine mounted on top of the boiler, and chains drove the rear wheels. Later came the 'under-type' which had the cylinders down at chassis level; one advantage of the under-type was that the driver could see where he was going better. Most wagons were the over-type like the two shown here.

STEAM AFLOAT

Jonathan Hulls (clearly an optimist) had the idea of using one of Newcomen's massive beam engines to drive a paddlewheel ship in 1736, but nothing came of it. Other experimenters dabbled with steamship designs through the 1770s with little more to show for their efforts.

Yet in the end it *was* something rather like a beam engine that powered the first commercially successful ship the 'Comet'. But the 'beam' was put down very low and became known as a 'side lever'. In practice, this kind of engine had two side levers acting together.

SIDE RODS
PISTON ROD
PADDLEWHEEL
SIDE LEVERS
FIXED PIVOT
CRANKSHAFT

THE SHIP THAT SHOULD HAVE BEEN THE FIRST SUCCESS

A ship that deserved success without achieving it was the Charlotte Dundas, which managed to pull two barges against a strong wind for nearly 20 miles in 1802 – about the time Trevithick's first locomotive appeared. But the Charlotte Dundas was said by the greybeards to break up canal banks with her wash, was laid up, and finally scrapped in 1861. Such lack of foresight seems astounding today.

THE SHIP THAT WAS THE FIRST SUCCESS

The Comet carried passengers on the Clyde from Glasgow to Greenock and back. She had an upright cylinder and side levers – as shown in the sketch. The funnel also acted as a mast for the mainsail.

She steamed successfully in around the Clyde until she ran aground in 1820 and became a total wreck.

STEAM AND THE HIGH SPEED

Soon marine engineers settled for two main types of engine: those designed to drive paddle wheels, and those for propellers.

On paddle engines the cylinders rest on the bottom of the ship facing diagonally up to the crankshaft on which the paddle wheels are fixed. On screw engines the cylinders are placed *above* the crankshaft which is directly coupled to the propeller shaft.

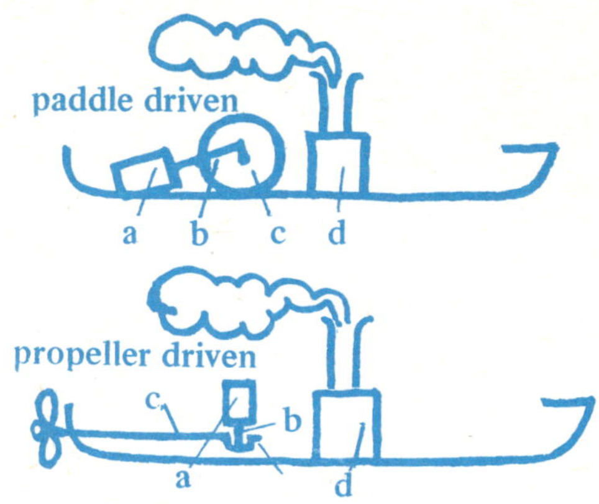

a cylinder with pistons
b piston rods and con rods
c crankshaft
d boiler to make steam

By 1880 large ships were being build, the hulls of iron and later of steel. Immense power was developed even in small ships – the tugs. Sails, which hac been thought necessary to help the engines began to disappear.

The 'Ryde' was built in 1937 for the (then) Southern Railway. She was the last of their paddle steamers and steamed between Portsmouth, Southsea and Ryde. She weighed 566 tons and carried 1011 passengers.

Engine room shot, paddle steamer 'Ryde'. These are triple expansion engines – meaning the steam exhausts from the first cylinder through two others, each cylinder larger than the previous one, to allow for the constantly expanding steam.

Photos: Michael Blenkinsop

Photo: CEGB

TURBINE

In a power station electro magnets in each generator are turned by engines called 'prime movers' to make electricity. Steam driven turbines are used to make 98% of Britain's electricity in this way. Steam is produced from water heated by burning coal or oil or by nuclear fission. High pressure steam is passed through the turbines and then enters a condenser where it passes over tubes containing cooling water. It is thus condensed back into water and creates a vacuum which helps improve the flow of steam through the turbines. The water is then returned to the boiler by a series of pumps.

The huge turbine hall at the Central Electricity Board's Cottam Power Station near Retford in Nottinghamshire. The 2,000 MW coal-fired power station contains four 500 MW turbo-generator units.

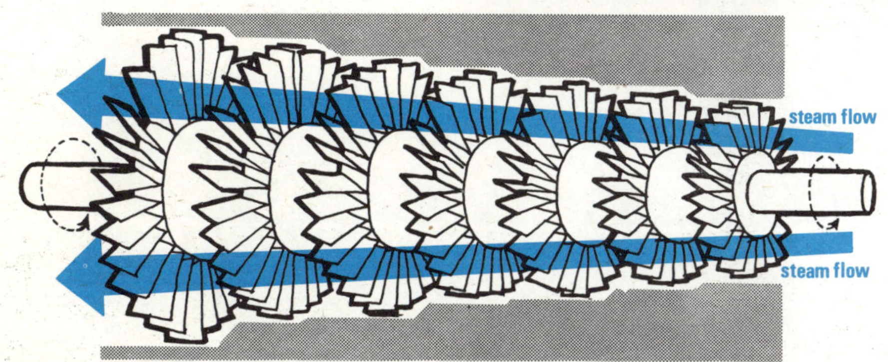

A turbine works like a windmill: the steam pushes against the wheel blades so that they turn round on their shaft. Larger wheels are set behind each other, allowing the expanded steam to use up every ounce of pressure.

Seamen were astounded when the first turbine driven ship, the Turbina, clocked up 34½ knots (about 40 miles per hour) in 1897.

Large ocean liners like the Queen Elizabeth could carry several thousand passengers and tiny steam launches only maybe 20 – but all were powered by steam.

After piston engines for paddles and screws came the giant step forward – the TURBINE, the work of the inventors de Laval, a Swede and an Englishman, Charles A Parsons. Turbine engines were not only used to power ships at high speed but became the main means of converting steam into electrical power.

Power for ships – the timetable

From about 1812 coal fired boilers driving paddles
From about 1840 the screw propeller
From about 1900 steam turbines and oil fired boilers
Today, nuclear power – but still using steam

The QE2 – world's most luxurious ship. She has two main engines each with a high pressure and a low pressure turbine – steam driven. The engines together develop 110 000 shaft horsepower. Her cruising speed is 29 knots and flat out speed 32 knots, 37 mph.

Photo: Cunard

HOW HIGH QUALITY WORKING STEAM MODELS ARE MADE

Working steam models are rather more than toys, and safety considerations alone require that they be very well made and thoroughly tested.

The photographs here show the Mamod range of steam powered engines – the stationary engines, wagon, tractor, roller and veteran car. They use solid fuel in place of the former methylated spirits and are extremely safe.

One of the most popular of the models is the realistic traction engine – and here is how it is built. The other models are made in a broadly similar way and with the same care.

THE TRACTION ENGINE
The materials used in the traction engine are the sturdy traditional ones: steel, brass, copper, zinc alloy and solder – and, of course, heat resistant, spray-coated paint and lacquers.

Manufacturing is separated out into short production lines, the engine building up stage by stage to completion as the many parts are prepared and assembled.

BOILERS
The brass boilers are bought in from specialist manufacturers already partly formed. They come as a complete cup (more like a narrow drinking glass in shape), pressed out from a single billet of brass. One end is open.

MAMOD BOILERS ARE TESTED TO 80 lbs sq in ALTHOUGH THE SAFETY VALVE 'BLOWS' AT ONLY 15 lbs AND THE ENGINE'S NORMAL WORKING PRESSURE IS ABOUT 10 lbs. SO THE SAFETY FACTOR IS ENORMOUS.

DRILLING AND SOLDERING
Many holes have to be formed in a steam engine. In the traction engine they have to be pierced to take the overflow plug, safety valve and whistle for a start. The overflow hole at the rear of the boiler has to be threaded, and the other two fitted with pre-threaded inserts; these inserts are fixed by a cleverly devised machine, the spin rivetter which puts them in and flattens and spreads them under the boiler's top (like rivetting), so that they never come out. It does so without damaging the threads. Then the whistle and safety valve can be simply screwed in, which happens later.

To complete the boiler, its open end must be closed. Liquid solder and flux is painted on the boiler rim and the endpiece fitted to it. Solder is painted round the inserts for the safety valve and whistle too, to be sure of steam proof joints, and the whole assembly passed through a very high temperature oven. Out comes a complete boiler ready for painting, or polishing and lacquering.

But we havent finished with hole drilling yet. Holes are required for the steam pipes, and very small ones for the 'engine faces'. Engine faces are the brass engine frame and the brass block forming a flat side to the cylinder and swinging up and down against the frame as the piston moves. The flat block acts as a valve taking steam from a hole in the engine frame and letting it through a hole drilled in itself to the cylinder. The steam coming through powers the piston. Other tiny matched holes let the used steam escape along a copper pipe to the chimney.

Mamod's traction engine and road roller with accessories.

The fit of the flat engine frame to the flat block on the side of the cylinder must be very accurate or steam will escape. This is done on an automatic machine.

THE DIE-CAST PARTS
Wheels, flywheels and the smokebox (the round piece on the front) and